AF605703

ADELAIDE
CAPITAL CITIES ACROSS AUSTRALIA
WILLIAM DAY
REDBACK
publishing

Redback Publishing
PO Box 357 Frenchs Forest NSW 2086
Australia

www.redbackpublishing.com.au
orders@redbackpublishing.com.au

978-1-925860-46-7

Author: William Day
Editor: Marianne Lindsell
Designer: Redback Publishing

Original illustrations © Redback Publishing 2019
Originated by Redback Publishing

Printed and bound in China by Leo Paper

Acknowledgements
Abbreviations: l—left, r—right, b—bottom, t—top, c—centre, m—middle
We would like to thank the following for permission to reproduce photographs: (Images © shutterstock), p3 Adelaide Oval, by Trentino Priori [CC BY-SA 3.0 (https://creativecommons.org/licenses/by-sa/3.0)], via Wikimedia commons, p6b Kangaroo Island kangaroos, by Paul Asman and Jill Lenoble under Creative commons, via Wikimedia commons, p8m "Settlement in South Australia" [B 45434], Photograph, State Library of South Australia, [Public Domain], p9b Governor John Hindmarsh, by Diceman [Public domain], via Wikimedia commons, p9tr George Jones (died 1869) [Public domain], via Wikimedia commons, p9m Charles Hill - The Proclamation of South Australia 1836 - Google Art Project, Art Gallery of South Australia [Public domain], via Wikimedia commons, p14 Adelaide Chinatown, Scott W. [CC BY-SA 3.0 (http://creativecommons.org/licenses/by-sa/3.0/)], via Wikimedia commons, p14l German settled village, George French Angas [Public domain], via Wikimedia commons, p15t St. Mary of the Cross, M.O.X [CC BY-SA 4.0 (https://creativecommons.org/licenses/by-sa/4.0)], via Wikimedia commons, p15b Irish potato famine Bridget O'Donnel, Illustrated London News, December 22, 1849 [Public domain], via Wikimedia commons, p16b Adelaide Town Hall, by corbs83 [CC BY 2.0 (https://creativecommons.org/licenses/by/2.0)], via Wikimedia comons, p17 Government House, Adelaide, 1865 , by Samuel White Sweet [Public domain], via Wikimedia commons, p17b Adelaide Coat of Arms, by www.civicheraldry.com [Public domain], via Wikimedia commons, p19m Sea princess 1720 (10260289264) (5), by Noel Jones [CC BY-SA 2.0 (https://creativecommons.org/licenses/by-sa/2.0)], via Wikimedia commons, p22b Camel Train offloading wool at a train station, South Australia, 1928, [Public domain], via Wikimedia commons, p28b Womadelaide 2011-2, Nichollas Harrison [CC BY-SA 3.0 (https://creativecommons.org/licenses/by-sa/3.0)], via Wikimedia commons.

A catalogue record for this book is available from the National Library of Australia

CONTENTS

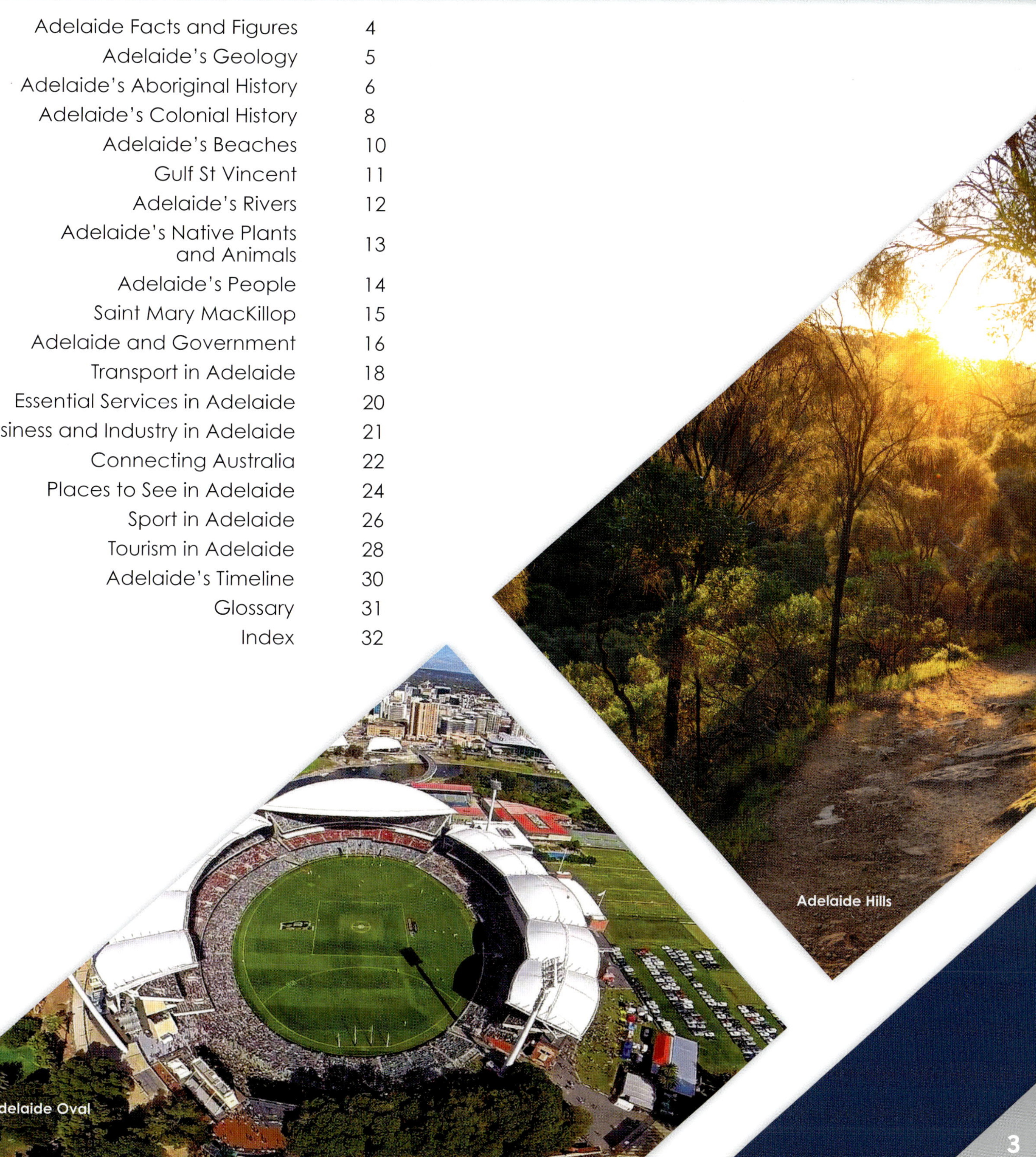

Adelaide Hills

Adelaide Oval

ADELAIDE FACTS & FIGURES

Adelaide is the capital city of South Australia. Located on the coastline of Gulf St Vincent, Adelaide was named after Queen Adelaide, wife of King William IV, who was the British monarch at the time the town was founded. Adelaide is one of the rare planned cities in Australia. Canberra, Australia's capital city, is another. Both had streets, services and locations of main buildings all planned before any building began.

Greater Adelaide extends from the coast and Gulf St Vincent in the west, across to the Adelaide Plains and the Adelaide Hills in the east.

Population in 2016

City of Adelaide – about 25,000 people

Greater Adelaide – about 1.3 million people

Height above sea level – from 0 metres at sea level to 727 metres at Mount Lofty

Area of Greater Adelaide – 3,258 square kilometres

Climate – temperate, Mediterranean-style climate

When people refer to Adelaide they could mean any one of five different areas

1. The city centre
2. The city centre plus its surrounding suburbs
3. The GCCSA
4. The local government area only
5. A personal idea of where they think the city is

Greater Capital City Statistical Areas (GCCSA)

The Australian Bureau of Statistics (ABS) collects data based on GCCSAs for each capital city around Australia. The GCCSA is not the same as the local government area that bears the name of the city. These GCCSAs can change if the ABS believes a city has grown beyond its previous boundaries. This means that statistics for population and economic activity will be different depending on whether the agency compiling them is describing the GCCSA, the local government area or some other definition they have for the extent of the city.

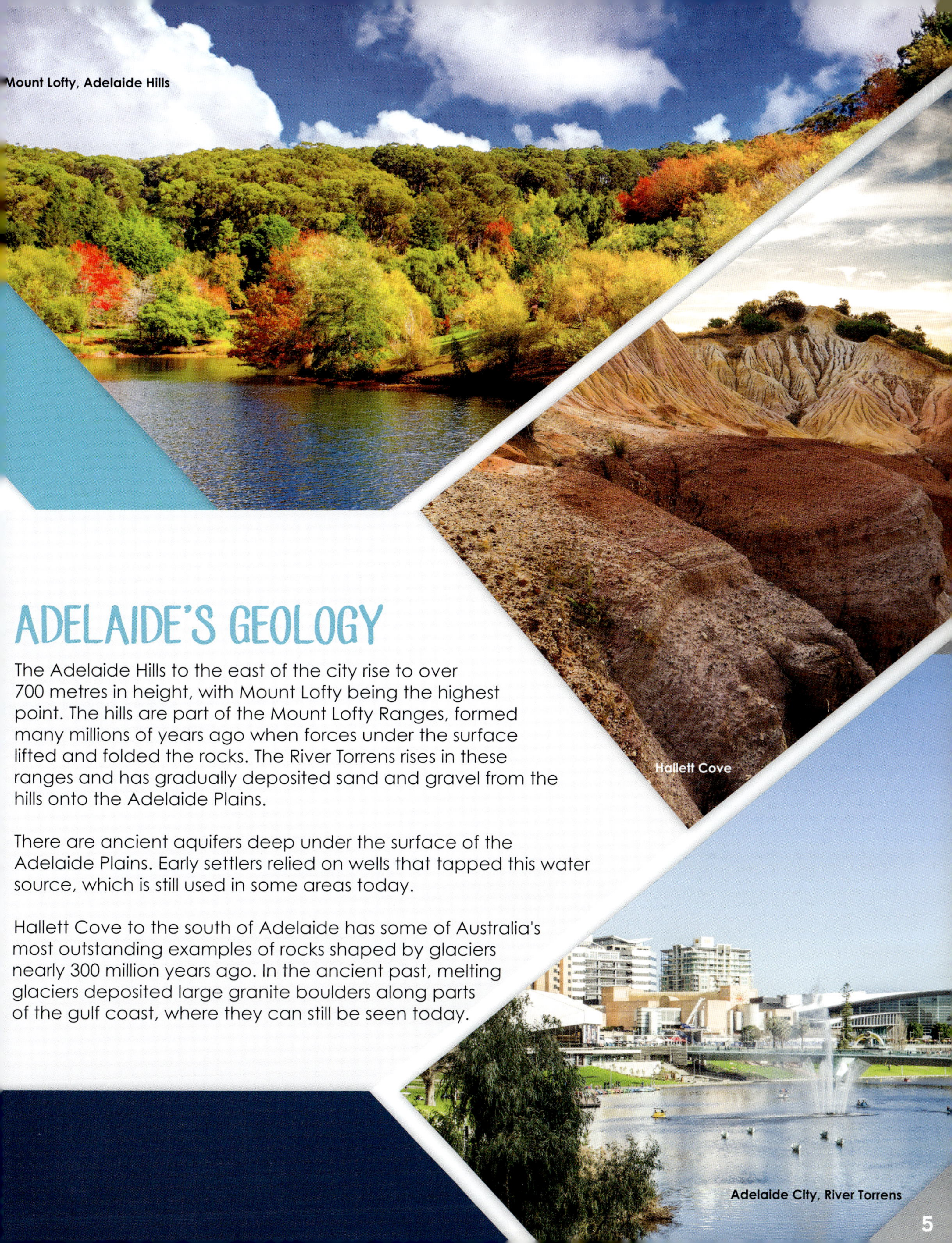

Mount Lofty, Adelaide Hills

Hallett Cove

Adelaide City, River Torrens

ADELAIDE'S GEOLOGY

The Adelaide Hills to the east of the city rise to over 700 metres in height, with Mount Lofty being the highest point. The hills are part of the Mount Lofty Ranges, formed many millions of years ago when forces under the surface lifted and folded the rocks. The River Torrens rises in these ranges and has gradually deposited sand and gravel from the hills onto the Adelaide Plains.

There are ancient aquifers deep under the surface of the Adelaide Plains. Early settlers relied on wells that tapped this water source, which is still used in some areas today.

Hallett Cove to the south of Adelaide has some of Australia's most outstanding examples of rocks shaped by glaciers nearly 300 million years ago. In the ancient past, melting glaciers deposited large granite boulders along parts of the gulf coast, where they can still be seen today.

ADELAIDE'S ABORIGINAL HISTORY

The Traditional Owners of the Adelaide Plains area and the site of the City of Adelaide are the Kaurna Aboriginal people.

Kaurna Shield

The City of Adelaide uses an image of a Kaurna shield, or wokali, on signage throughout its parks. The image is based on an actual wokali which is kept by the city as a treasured item from Adelaide's past. The shield is about 150 years old and it would have been used by a Kaurna man.

Land Management With Fire

Much of the Adelaide Plains was covered with grass at the time of first European settlement. This grassland was probably the result of Aboriginal methods of land clearing. Using controlled fires, they kept grassed areas lush and avoided catastrophic bushfires. The open grassland made hunting easier and encouraged kangaroos to come and graze.

Kaurna Children and German Missionaries

In the 1830s, German missionaries opened a school for Kaurna children and taught them using the Kaurna language. This continued for a number of years until Governor Grey closed their school. The teachers compiled a grammar and dictionary of the Kaurna language, and translated Bible passages and Christian hymns into Kaurna. Examples of the children's school work still exist, showing the Kaurna language written in perfect 19th century handwriting.

Nakutha!

Niina Marni?

Marni tirntu!

Paitya!

Panyi marni!

Kangaroo Island kangaroos

Statue of Queen Victoria, erected in 1894 at Victoria Square

Place Names

Kaurna place names are reappearing in Adelaide, as local government pursues a policy of dual naming and reinstatement of original names. The River Torrens now has the dual name of Karrawirra Parri, which means 'Redgum Forest River', and Victoria Square has the dual name Tarntanyangga, which means 'Red Kangaroo Dreaming'.

Aboriginal Flag

Victoria Square / Tarntanyangga in Adelaide has the honour of being the place in Australia where the Aboriginal Flag flew for the first time. Designed by Harold Thomas, the flag was raised in Victoria Square / Tarntanyangga in July 1971 in support of land rights for Aboriginal people. Since 1995, the flag has been flown as one of Australia's official flags. While permission from the government is needed to fly some of Australia's official flags, this is not the case with the Aboriginal Flag.

ADELAIDE'S COLONIAL HISTORY

Adelaide was founded as a carefully planned city, designed to attract free settlers. Unlike other colonies on the Australian continent, Adelaide was to be free of Britain's transported convicts.

Settlers

In 1834, the British parliament passed an Act which allowed settlers to make their new homes in the colony of South Australia. Shortly afterwards, the South Australian Company, formed by a group of London entrepreneurs, began promoting land in South Australia and encouraging emigrants from Britain to consider settling there. They advertised the new colony as a perfect destination for families wanting to start a new life in the Australian colonies. The emigrants were promised the possibility of eventually being able to buy plots of land in a destination which was to be free from the negative outcomes that convict transportation had caused in Australia's other colonies. The hopeful settlers were not fully aware that there would be no facilities for them in the new colony. After arriving, they lived in tents and huts, drew water from the river in buckets, and experienced harsh conditions as they cleared land and began farming. All imported supplies came from ships which arrived at Port Adelaide. People and their goods then had to travel the lengthy distance to the town further inland.

Early settlement in South Australia

William Light

A convoy of ships full of new settlers arrived in 1836. The surveyor of the land, William Light, came before them and began laying out the streets and plots of land. He landed at Rapid Bay, where he carved his initials into a boulder which is now in the South Australian Museum.

William Light sited Adelaide a short distance up the River Torrens, rather than right on the shore of Gulf St Vincent. His choice of this location meant that there was further to transport goods into the centre of Adelaide when ships arrived at ports on the coast. However, the provision of clean water for drinking was more important, and locating the settlement further upstream meant that the water supply would not be contaminated by saltwater flowing up with the tides.

William Light

The Proclamation of Adelaide

Governor Hindmarsh

John Hindmarsh was the first Governor of South Australia. He arrived in 1836 as part of the convoy that brought the early settlers. He insisted that the new town of Adelaide must have a port, and instructed William Light to survey land which became Port Adelaide.

ADELAIDE'S BEACHES

Greater Adelaide has a long coastline with many beaches, cliffs and headlands. Jetties which extend into the gulf waters are a feature of this coastline.

Semaphore Beach

Semaphore, which dates from the 1850s, prides itself on its historic buildings. The Time Ball Tower, built in 1875, was originally used by sailors to determine the exact time. A black ball, dropped at precisely 1pm each day, signalled ships to check their chronometers and vital navigation instruments. Today, the black ball still drops at 1pm every day.

Sellicks Beach

At the southern edge of the Greater Adelaide region, Sellicks Beach is a good choice for people who want to get away from the crowds.

Port Noarlunga

Although no longer used as a port for shipping, the beach and jetty are tourist attractions at Port Noarlunga. At low tide, visitors to the jetty can easily see the exposed reef.

Aldinga Beach

Cars are allowed to drive along and park on this beach, while the walking trails at Aldinga Scrub Conservation Park offer dunes, rare orchids and the chance to see echidnas and birdlife.

Brighton Beach

A long beach with a jetty. Popular with Adelaide's city residents, Brighton Beach is the venue for an annual sculpture exhibition.

Henley Beach

Henley Beach is very close to Adelaide, making it a favourite with locals.

Glenelg Beach

A convenient tram ride from the centre of Adelaide, Glenelg is a resort-style beach suburb.

GULF ST VINCENT

Gulf St Vincent is one of two large gulfs along the South Australian coast. Over many thousands of years, the sea level has changed a number of times, resulting in Gulf St Vincent being dry land at some times and covered with water at others.

Investigations by British explorers in the early 1800s noted that the gulf was a possible site for a safe harbour, as it would allow ships to escape dangerous weather conditions in the ocean further south.

Gulf St Vincent is now a source of seafood for private and commercial fishers. It is also a location for recreational water sports and boating.

Habitats for Wildlife in Gulf St Vincent

- seagrass beds
- mangrove forests
- wetlands
- rock pools
- beaches

ADELAIDE'S RIVERS

River Torrens - Karrawirra Parri

When William Light was deciding where to locate the town of Adelaide, the course of the River Torrens was an important factor in his decision.

The River Torrens rises in the Adelaide Hills northeast of Adelaide, and empties into Gulf St Vincent. Urban stormwater runoff and silt now enter the gulf from the river, but this was not always the case. Before colonisation, the River Torrens flowed into a series of wetlands and used to fluctuate between flooding and drying out to a series of waterholes. In the 1800s, the construction of weirs to dam the river made the water supply more stable and created lakes. These weirs still provide water for the people of Adelaide, but only remnants of the wetlands still exist.

Gawler River

Flowing to the north of Adelaide, the Gawler River enters Gulf St Vincent at Port Gawler. The port was used to export the farm produce from the large Port Gawler estate, once owned by the son-in-law of South Australia's first Governor, John Hindmarsh.

Onkaparinga River

The name of the Onkaparinga River is based on the Kaurna word Ngangkiparingka, which refers to the river being a special place for women. The river rises in the Mount Lofty Ranges, meanders through the southern parts of Greater Adelaide and enters Gulf St Vincent at Port Noarlunga. Early European settlers farmed land beside the river and sent their produce on barges down to the coast. From there, the produce could be loaded onto ships and sent to markets in other colonies or overseas.

Onkaparinga River

ADELAIDE'S NATIVE PLANTS AND ANIMALS

The Adelaide Plains used to be covered with grasses, Blue Gums, Red Gums and Mallee trees. A vast range of plants existed in the more temperate conditions in the Adelaide Hills. These included ferns, orchids and lilies. Echidnas, bandicoots, wombats, possums and kangaroos were common and Kaurna people hunted them for food and skins. There were no koalas at the time of the European first settlement, but koalas were introduced to the forests later.

Endangered Mammals

Western Pygmy Possum

Grey-Headed Flying Fox

Southern Brown Bandicoot

There are many challenges to the continued survival of wildlife in urban Adelaide

- Loss of habitat
- Weeds
- Herbicides and pesticides
- Introduced and feral animals and plants
- Poor natural water quality
- Light and noise pollution
- Climate change
- Aggressive native birds, such as currawongs and noisy miners

Echidna

Kangaroo

ADELAIDE'S PEOPLE

Migration Museum

Settlement Square at Adelaide's Migration Museum is paved with the names of people who have travelled from overseas to make South Australia their home. The museum has collections and displays of precious historic items dating from the time of the colony's first settlers up to that of more recent migrants.

Chinese Settlers

Adelaide's Chinatown is near the Adelaide Central Market, which dates from 1869. Chinese market gardeners sold their produce at the markets, and began opening shops nearby. From these small beginnings, Chinatown grew into one of Adelaide's most visited tourist attractions.

During the Gold Rush after the 1850s, Chinese arrivals were not allowed to disembark at ports in other colonies. To overcome this, they landed at ports in South Australia instead and walked overland to the gold fields in Victoria.

Adelaide's Chinatown

German Settlers

Many descendants of the early German settlers are still living in Greater Adelaide. They migrated to the new colony of South Australia in the 1830s, seeking a place where they were free to practise their Lutheran religion without being persecuted. They settled throughout the countryside, building towns and churches, and became pioneers of South Australia's wine industry.

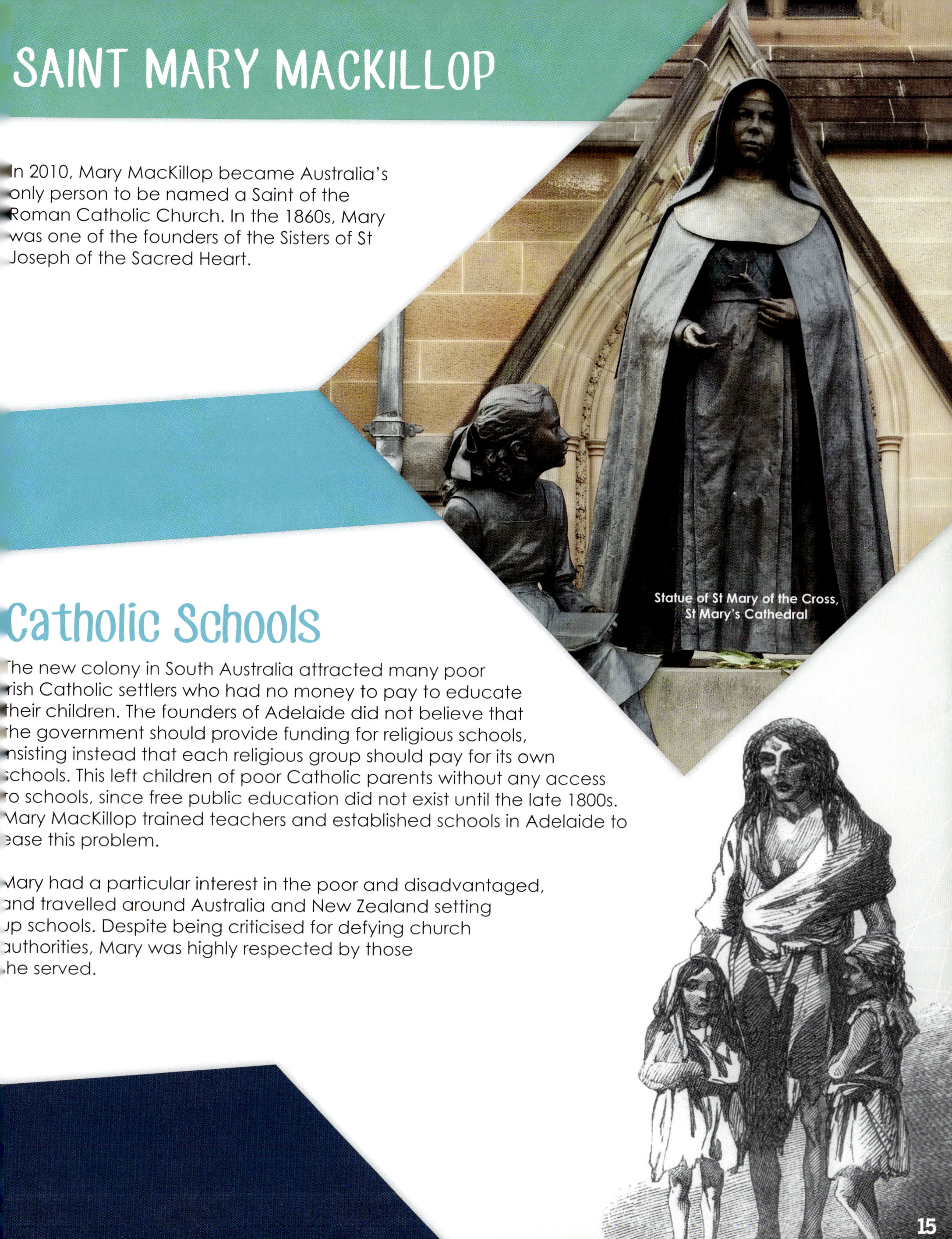

SAINT MARY MACKILLOP

In 2010, Mary MacKillop became Australia's only person to be named a Saint of the Roman Catholic Church. In the 1860s, Mary was one of the founders of the Sisters of St Joseph of the Sacred Heart.

Statue of St Mary of the Cross, St Mary's Cathedral

Catholic Schools

The new colony in South Australia attracted many poor Irish Catholic settlers who had no money to pay to educate their children. The founders of Adelaide did not believe that the government should provide funding for religious schools, insisting instead that each religious group should pay for its own schools. This left children of poor Catholic parents without any access to schools, since free public education did not exist until the late 1800s. Mary MacKillop trained teachers and established schools in Adelaide to ease this problem.

Mary had a particular interest in the poor and disadvantaged, and travelled around Australia and New Zealand setting up schools. Despite being criticised for defying church authorities, Mary was highly respected by those she served.

Adelaide City Council

The people of Adelaide were proud to be free of convicts in their settlement, and they were quick to demand an independent city council to look after their needs. Adelaide City Council is the oldest local government body in Australia. Created in 1840, the original council came into being only four years after the first settlers arrived in South Australia. The first mayor was James Fisher. The early councils were plagued with labour shortages and a lack of funds, but eventually improved their finances and were able to construct much needed roads and bridges.

Adelaide Town Hall

Opened in 1866, the Adelaide Town Hall, and the General Post Office across the street from it, remained the two tallest structures in Adelaide until more modern buildings rose above them in the 20th century.

Adelaide's Sister Cities

- Austin, Texas, USA (1983)
- Christchurch, New Zealand (1972)
- George Town, Malaysia (1973)
- Himeji, Japan (1982)
- Qingdao, China (2014)

Adelaide's Friendship Cities

- Dalian, China (2001)
- Chengdu, China (2001)

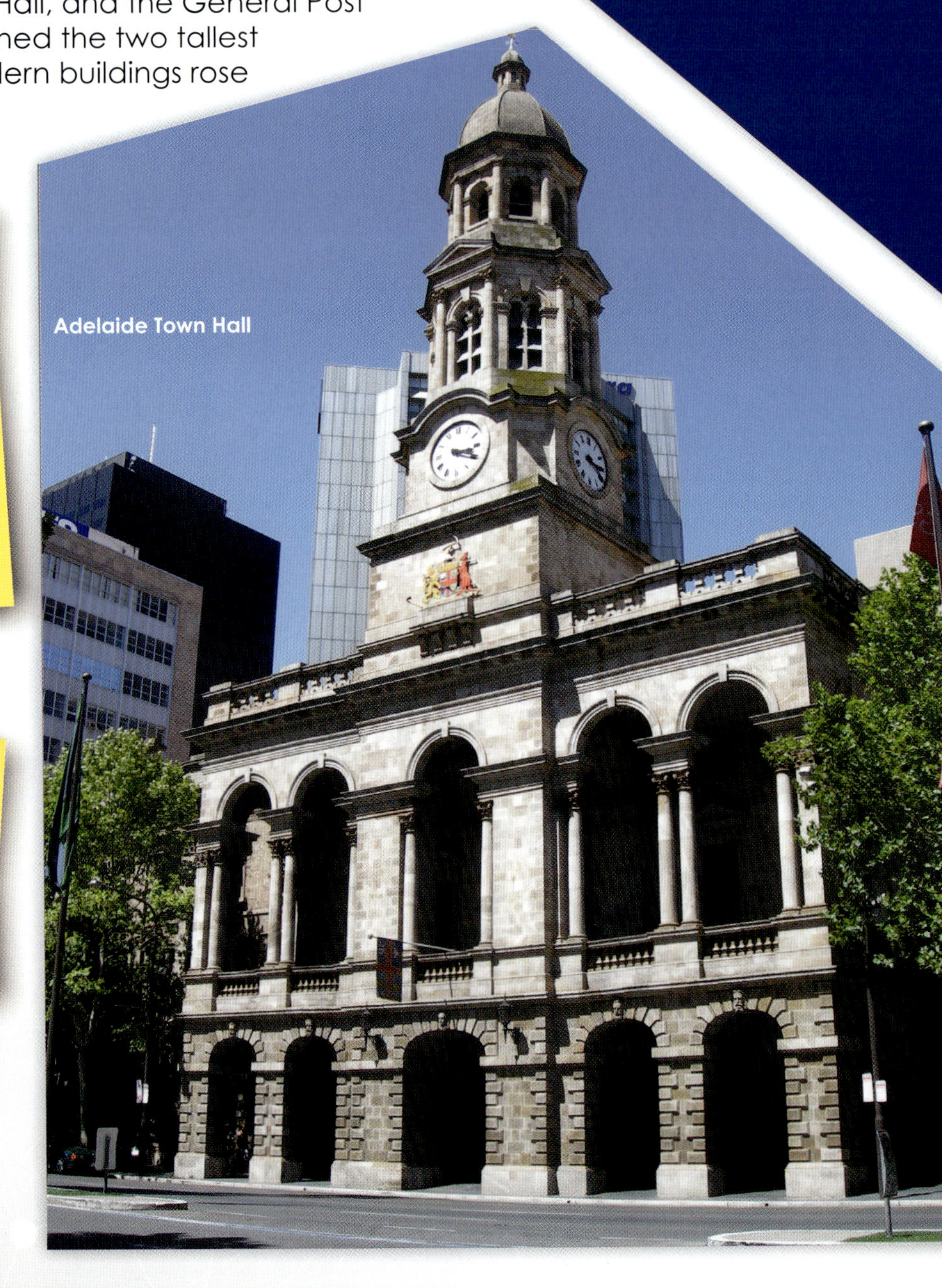

Adelaide Town Hall

Government House

The first Government House building was a simple slab hut. This was eventually replaced by a more permanent building. The new Government House was built in 1840, and has had a number of additions made to it since then. It has the distinction of being the oldest Government House in Australia that has been continuously occupied by the Governor.

Parliament of South Australia

The state parliament of South Australia meets in Parliament House in Adelaide. The imposing, colonnaded building was built in stages, the first being completed in 1889, and the second section fifty years later in 1939.

Government House 1865

Adelaide Coat of Arms

Red Kangaroo - The male red kangaroo is an important symbolic animal for the Kaurna people

Lion - A symbol of the British origins of the settlement

Miner's Pick - Refers to the importance of mining

Shield - Images on the shield refer to agriculture and shipping

TRANSPORT IN ADELAIDE

Adelaide Metro

Adelaide Metro is Adelaide's public transport system. Its services include buses, trains and trams that operate throughout Adelaide and its suburbs.

Trains

Passenger steam trains in Adelaide date from the 1850s. They were later replaced by diesel locomotives. Adelaide's electric train services only began running in 2014.

Adelaide is now an arrival and departure point for three of Australia's most famous long distance train journeys. They leave from the Adelaide Parklands Terminal and are operated by Great Southern Rail.

The Ghan (Adelaide - Alice Springs - Darwin)

The Indian Pacific (Perth - Adelaide - Sydney)

The Overland (Adelaide - Melbourne)

Green Travel

Green Travel means choosing travel options that are good for the environment. In Adelaide, Green Travel planning includes:

Smart Travel – choosing the best option

Car Share – short term rental instead of ownership

Electric Vehicles – private cars can use the charging stations installed in Adelaide.

Roads

Roads in the centre of Adelaide were all carefully laid out when the town was founded. However, roads out of Adelaide to other centres took many years to be built due to the shortage of workers to build them and the funds to pay for them.

Port Adelaide

Port Adelaide

Port Adelaide was created as the town's shipping port soon after the first settlement of Adelaide. It is still the main shipping port for goods passing in and out of Adelaide. A range of agricultural and mining produce leaves South Australia through Port Adelaide, and smaller items are carried in and out in container tankers. Port Adelaide also has berths for cruise shipping and provides facilities for tourists at the Port Adelaide Passenger Terminal.

Airport

Located at Hendon, not far from the city centre, Adelaide's first airport was built in the 1920s.

The current airport dates from the 1950s, when the passenger terminal was a very simple and uncomfortable building. International flights began operating in the 1980s when a new international passenger terminal was built.

The historic Vickers Vimy aircraft, flown by Keith and Ross Smith in the London to Australia air race of 1919, is kept as a museum display at the airport.

ESSENTIAL SERVICES IN ADELAIDE

Water

River Torrens

The River Torrens was Adelaide's first source of drinking water. Downstream, its waters are now fed by stormwater runoff, but weirs further upstream still help to supply Adelaide with water. Before homes had water supplied to them in pipes, the residents of Adelaide relied on water carters who filled tanks with river water and then sold it to householders.

Glenelg Adelaide Pipeline

Recycled water flows to Adelaide through the Glenelg Adelaide Pipeline. This water is used in the Park Lands.

Desalination

The Adelaide Desalination Plant began operation in 2011.

River Murray

Water from the River Murray has been pumped to Adelaide since the 1950s.

River Murray

Energy Production Timeline

1860s - street lightling by gas lamps

1890s - electricity supplied to parts of Adelaide area from local power stations

2000s - wind farms supply some of Adelaide's electricity

Sources Of Energy

Natural gas – South Australia's natural gas comes from plants in South Australia, Victoric and Queensland

Wind energy – South Australia is a large producer of wind energy

Solar cells – South Australia encourage its residents to install solar power cells

Diesel – Some power generation uses diesel as a fuel

BUSINESS AND INDUSTRY IN ADELAIDE

Within the City of Adelaide some of the main business types are:

- financial and business services
- the operations of government
- tourism and food services
- shops
- education services for international students

Central Market

Dating from 1869, when the city council established the town's first market, the Central Market is still a busy part of Adelaide.

Agriculture

Over half of the Greater Adelaide region is used for agriculture. Most farmers in the area graze livestock on pastures, or grow fruit, grapes for wine, or vegetables.

Commercial Fishing

Being located on Gulf St Vincent gives Adelaide a fishing industry right on its coastal border. Recreational and commercial fishers from the Greater Adelaide region collect and fish for whiting, snapper, blue crabs, giant crabs, western king prawns, southern rock lobsters and many more sought-after species. Commercial fishing in Gulf St Vincent is controlled by a management plan that protects the regions resources.

CONNECTING AUSTRALIA

Despite being so isolated from the other early colonies, Adelaide became an important centre for international and transcontinental communications. Both the Overland Telegraph Line and the first railway line to the north of Australia had their origins based in Adelaide. Both of these projects were major engineering feats and had profound effects on business and personal communications, both within Australia and with the rest of the world.

Aboriginal Australians

In the late 1800s, Aboriginal Australians who had cared for the desert and its precious water sources for thousands of years were suddenly subjected to an invasion of workers and camels. The newcomers and their animals destroyed water springs and cut paths through land where there were sacred sites and valuable food sources.

Afghan Cameleers

Horses or oxen were unsuited to the desert conditions, so thousands of camels were imported to carry the equipment needed to build the Overland Telegraph Line and the railway through the desert and savannah country. The Afghan cameleers and their camels were vital to the success of these two projects, which could not have been completed without them.

The Afghan cameleers have become legendary in the areas where they worked, although they were not all actually from Afghanistan. Some of the men were from India and Pakistan. After their work on the telegraph line and the railway was finished, some of the men returned to their homeland, while others settled in Australia and raised families. Their proud descendants live throughout South Australia. As well as leaving small, temporary mosques along the routes they travelled, the Afghan cameleers also built the first mosque in Adelaide. It dates from 1888 and is in Gilbert Street.

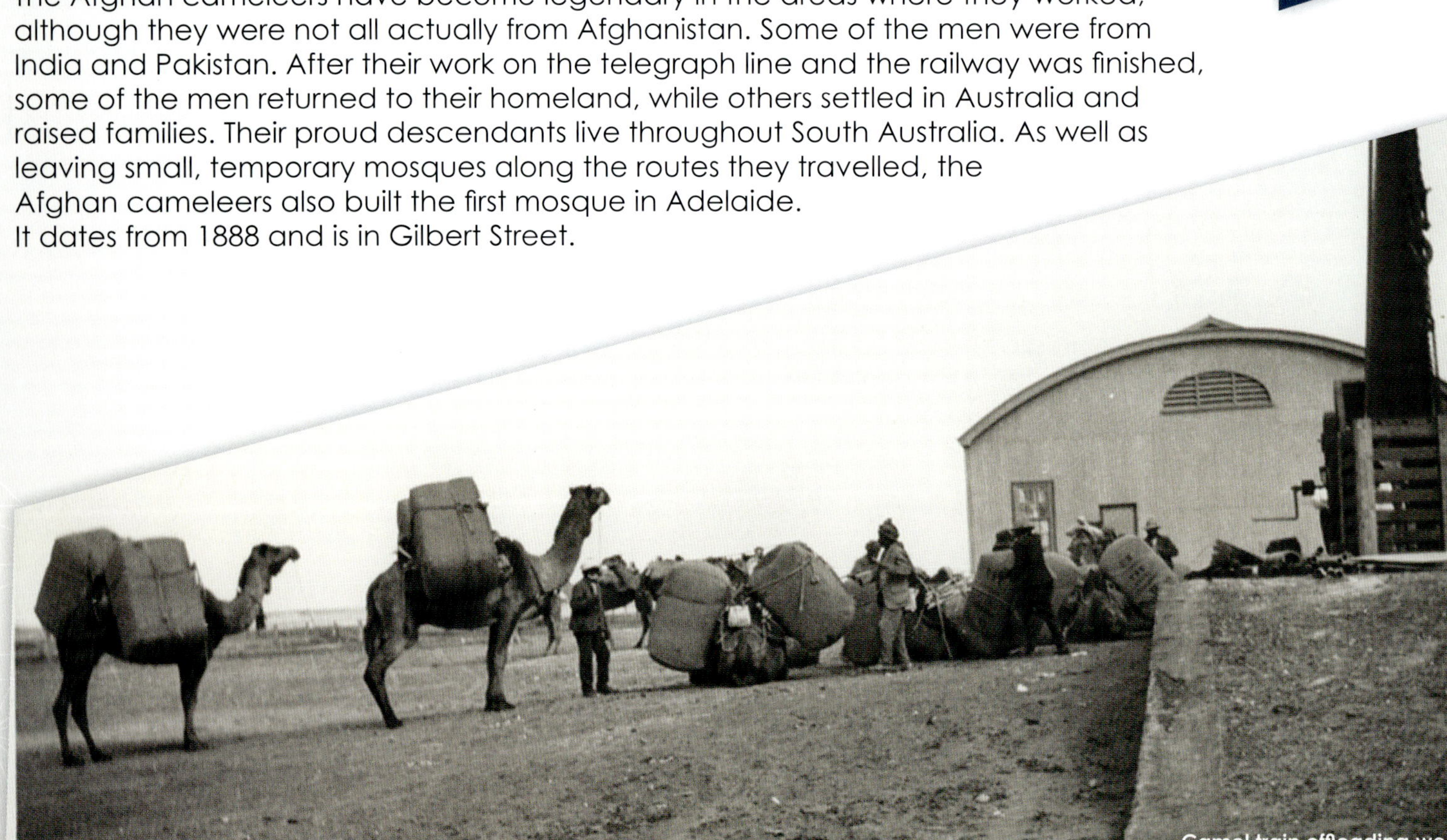

Camel train offloading wool

Overland Telegraph Line

For the European settlers in the 1800s, Australia was a very remote place to be. The only connection with Britain or other European countries was through sending letters on sailing ships. The deliveries took months to arrive.

The invention of the telegraph in the 1830s enabled messages to travel long distances by using Morse Code. A person would use a Morse Code machine to send the message as a series of dots and dashes. An operator at the receiving end translated the code back into words. The 'telegram boy' then used a bicycle to deliver the hand-written telegrams to homes and businesses.

Charles Todd

Appointed in 1855, Charles Todd was the first government Superintendent of Telegraphs. In 1870, he began the important task of managing the laying of a telegraph line across the vast distance between Adelaide and Darwin. It involved crossing deserts where there was little or no water, and much of the route was previously unexplored by any European person.

Laying the Telegraph Line

The Overland Telegraph Line was completed in just two years; a remarkable achievement considering a distance of 3,000 kilometres was involved. A telegraph line to the north was necessary because Darwin was the only place in Australia where the line from overseas came ashore. Adelaide received the very first message from overseas via the new telegraph line in 1872.

The Ghan Railway

The railway line that links Adelaide, Alice Springs and Darwin is now called The Ghan, in honour of the Afghan cameleers who helped to build it.

The railway connected the southern colonies with the remote north of Australia. Without it, the most practical and cheapest way to transport people or goods from the south to the north was by ship around the coast.

Construction of the line began in 1878. Unlike the Overland Telegraph Line, which was completed in record time, the railway from Adelaide to Darwin was not finished until 2004. In its early years, the railway was often damaged by floods.

Steam trains needed a supply of water along the route, but the minerals in the bore water used caused problems in the steam engines. Water use along the route created a source of conflict with the Aboriginal people, who protested that their water springs and wells were being damaged.

The privately owned Ghan now offers one of the world's great rail journeys.

PLACES TO SEE IN ADELAIDE

- Adelaide Botanic Garden
- Adelaide Central Market
- Adelaide Convention Centre
- Adelaide Festival Centre
- Adelaide Gaol
- Adelaide Park Lands
- Adelaide Zoo
- Art Gallery of South Australia
- Chinatown
- Cleland Wildlife Park
- Glenelg Beach
- Government House
- Hahndorf
- Migration Museum
- Montefiore Hill
- Mount Lofty
- Parliament House
- River Torrens
- Riverbank Precinct
- Rundle Mall
- South Australian Museum

Adelaide Gaol

The Adelaide Gaol is one of the oldest remaining colonial public buildings in Adelaide. Work on it began in 1840 and it was closed as a jail in 1988. It is now a museum of crime and punishment in Adelaide. Saint Mary MacKillop, who founded the Sisters of St Joseph of the Sacred Heart, was a frequent visitor to the inmates at Adelaide Gaol.

Adelaide Zoo

The only Giant Pandas in Australia live at Adelaide Zoo.

Mount Lofty

Mount Lofty is the highest place in Greater Adelaide.

Adelaide Park Lands

Adelaide Park Lands form a large green border to the city centre. They are a refuge for city workers and residents, where they can relax, play sport, ride bicycles, walk their dog or just enjoy nature.

The Park Lands are a legacy left to the people of Adelaide by William Light, who planned the layout of the early town in 1837. He also allowed in his design for city squares, which is the origin of Victoria Square in Adelaide. The extent of the Park Lands was under threat on a number of occasions, as people used the land for dumping rubbish, for quarrying and as locations for government structures and other buildings. There are some remnant bush areas in the Park Lands where visitors can imagine how the Adelaide Plains would have looked before colonisation.

Giant Panda

Adelaide Park Lands

River Torrens bike track

SPORT IN ADELAIDE

Adelaide Cup

The Adelaide Cup is a horse race that runs every year on the second Monday in March. This day has been a public holiday in Adelaide since 1973. People dress in their best clothes and gather to celebrate together at the racecourse, while others take advantage of the long weekend to enjoy a short vacation.

The first Adelaide Cup race was held at Thebarton Racecourse in 1864 and attracted thousands of people. The winner received 500 guineas, which was an extremely large amount of money at the time. In the years that followed, the location of the race changed to Victoria Park Racecourse and in 1876 to Morphettville Racecourse, where it is still held today.

Adelaide Oval

Close to the centre of the city and with easy access to it from all directions, the Adelaide Oval is the city's major venue for sporting and large concert events.

As well as visiting the oval for sporting events or spectacular concerts, those who are not afraid of heights can take the Roof Climb experience. Clambering across the very top of the stadium, fifty metres above the ground, intrepid climbers are rewarded with unique views of both Adelaide and the oval below.

Adelaide Oval dates from 1871, when it was established to provide a venue for cricket matches.

Adelaide 500

The Adelaide 500 is an annual Supercar racing event. The course includes closed Adelaide streets and parts of the Park Lands. Some sections of the course were formerly used for the Australian Grand Prix motor race. The early years of competition included modified streetcars made by Ford and Holden and the first winner of the event was Craig Lowndes in 1999.

Craig Lowndes

As well as the race, the Adelaide 500 also provides a range of other forms of entertainment for those who attend. Music concerts, displays and special attractions for children make the Adelaide 500 a family-friendly event.

Adelaide Clipsal 500

South Australian Sport Hall of Fame and Legends

Each year since 2010, Sport SA takes nominations for those outstanding athletes who should be included in the Hall of Fame. The winners are announced at a function held at the Adelaide Oval. Membership represents the highest level of recognition for a South Australian athlete.

TOURISM IN ADELAIDE

Visitor Information

The Adelaide Visitor Information Centre and the Adelaide Greeters Service provide tourists with information on making their way around the city. The Adelaide Greeters Service is provided by enthusiastic volunteers whose aim is to make travellers' visits to Adelaide as uncomplicated as possible.

Adelaide Festival

Since the first Adelaide Festival in 1960, this event has showcased artists, writers, musicians and performers. Held at a variety of venues throughout Adelaide, including the Adelaide Festival Centre, the program attracts both locals and visitors to the city.

Hahndorf

On the far outskirts of the Greater Adelaide area is Hahndorf, one of the most interesting towns in Australia. Hahndorf is a little piece of Germany in the Adelaide Hills. The German migrants who founded it in the late 1830s were looking for a country where they could practise their religion freely and without persecution. They found that place in Australia and began to build a village which still retains its German style. The famous Australian artist, Hans Heysen, lived and worked in Hahndorf, and his house is now a museum.

Self-Guided Walks

Self-guided walks around Adelaide's historic sites take tourists on interesting and sometimes surprising journeys that reveal stories about the old town and its people.

Fishing in Gulf St Vincent

Being located on the coast gives people in Adelaide easy access to great fishing spots in Gulf St Vincent. Fishers take their fishing rods to the beaches at Glenelg, Henley Beach and Semaphore and fish from boats, the coast and jetties in their search for the best catch. There are regulations about protected species, equipment and catch sizes to ensure the sustainability of the resources.

WOMADelaide

WOMADelaide is an outdoor event featuring music, food, stalls and entertainment. Held annually in Botanic Park in Adelaide, it is a destination for music lovers from all around Australia. The name is based on WOMAD, World of Music and Dance, a festival organisation.

UNESCO Creative Cities Network

In 2015, Adelaide received the honour of becoming the first UNESCO City of Music in Australia, due to its commitment to music education and performance. The aim of the Creative Cities Network is to encourage the development of culture and creativity worldwide. Adelaide's Elder Conservatorium is Australia's oldest tertiary music school, dating from 1883.

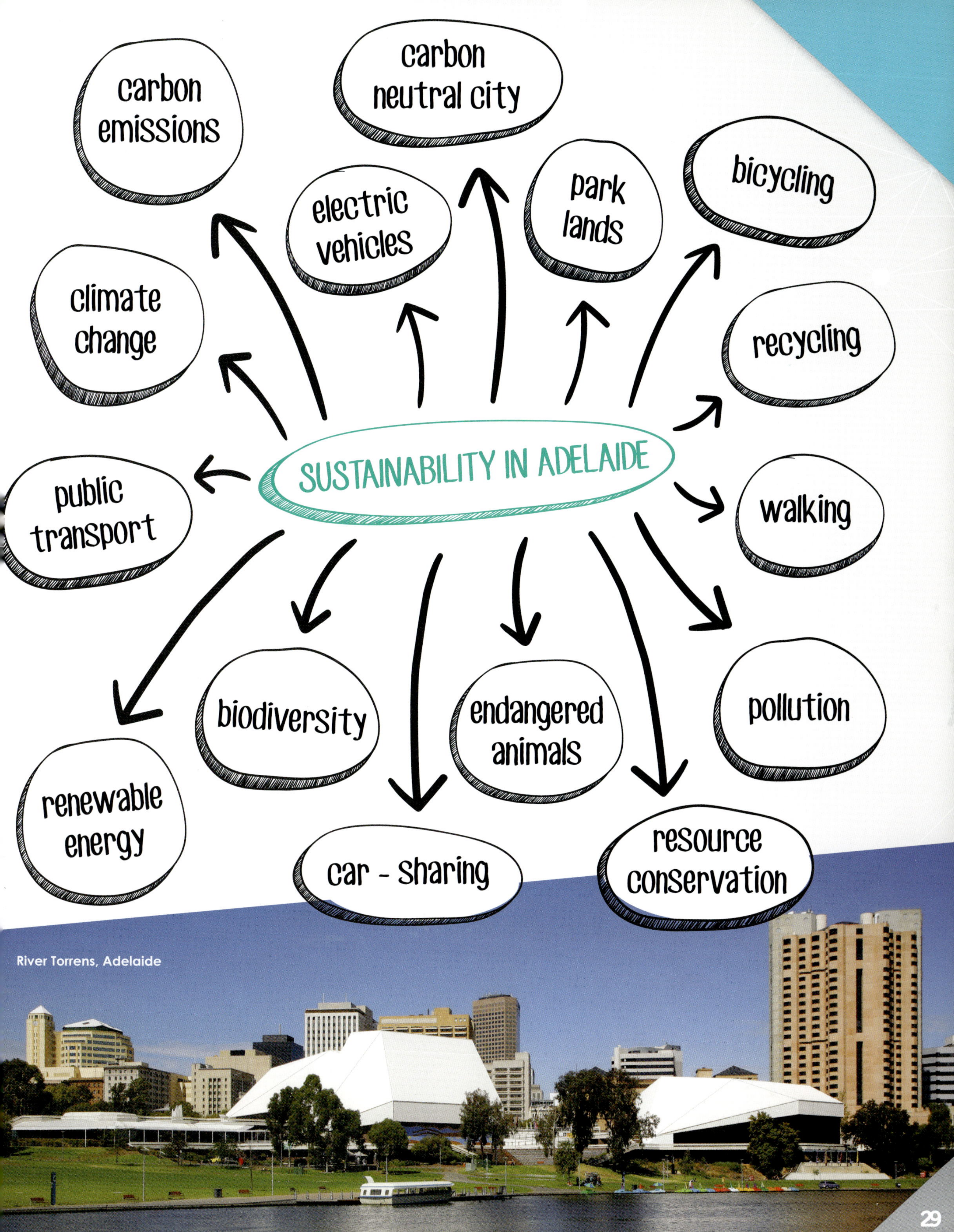

River Torrens, Adelaide

ADELAIDE'S TIMELINE

300 million years ago
Glaciers covered parts of Adelaide

02

Thousands of years ago
Australian Aboriginal people lived in the Adelaide area

1802
Matthew Flinders made charts of the coast of Gulf St Vincent

1834
Britain passed an Act of Parliament allowing settlement in South Australia

1836
First European settlers arrived in Adelaide

06

1840
Adelaide's first local government formed

1866
Adelaide Town Hall built

1869
First city market opened

1872
Australia's first telegraph message from overseas was received in Adelaide

1878
First horse-drawn trams in Adelaide

11

1894
South Australia became the first place in Australia to allow women to vote and to stand for election to parliament

1901
Federation made Adelaide the capital of the State of South Australia

13

1971
Aboriginal Flag flown in Adelaide for the first time anywhere in Australia

Horse-drawn tram returns from Granite Island, Victor Harbor

aquifer natural underground water source

colonist person who settles in a new land and imposes their own culture on it

continuously without interruption

disembark leave a method of transport

entrepreneur person who starts a business

geology study of rocks and how they form the Earth

glacier mass of slow-moving ice

quarrying cutting stones out of the ground

transportation taking of convicts from Britain to the Australian colonies

weir water reservoir

Port Willunga Jetty

INDEX

Wisteria Lane in the Adelaide Botanic Garden